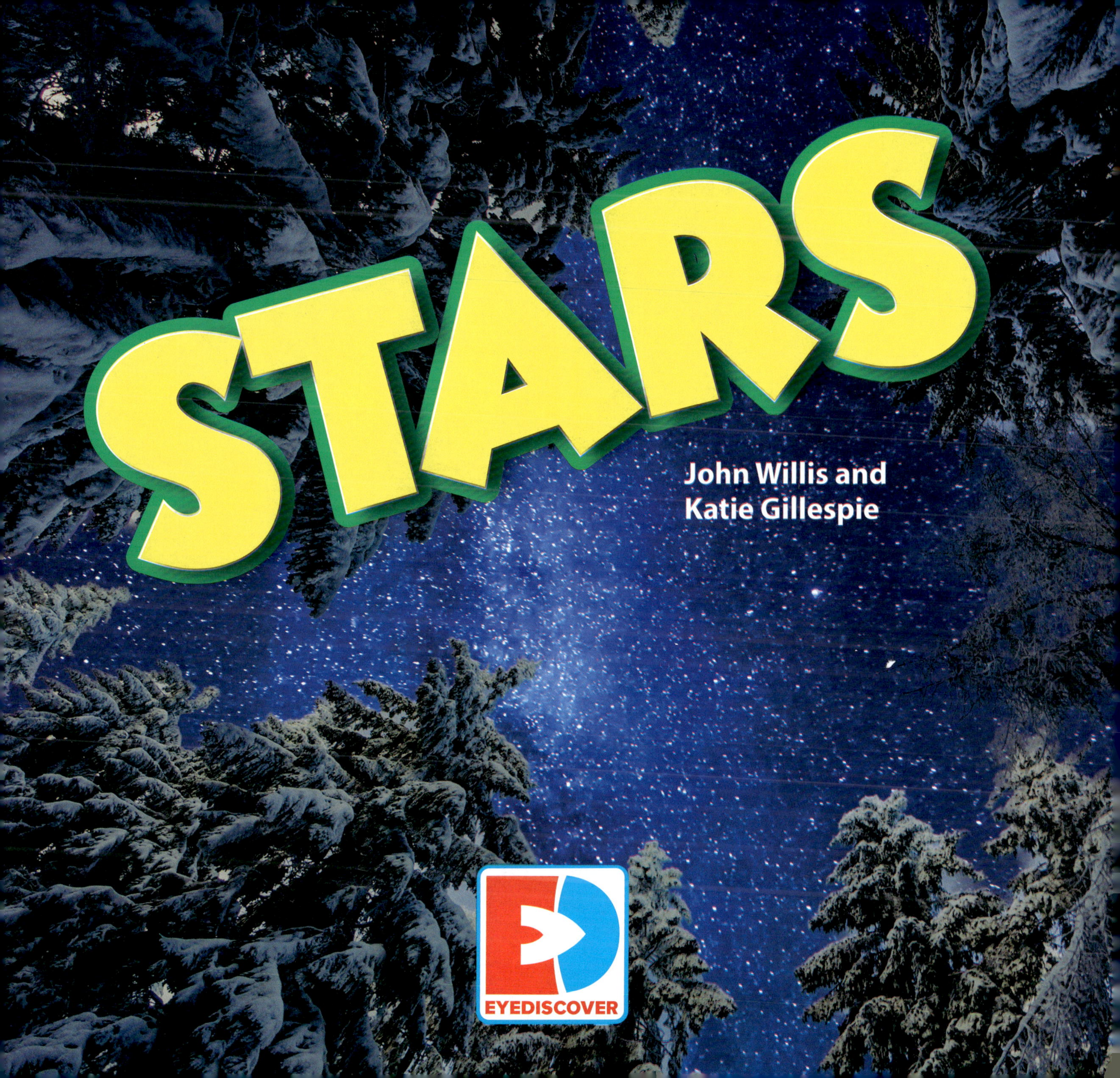
STARS
John Willis and
Katie Gillespie
EYEDISCOVER

Go to **www.eyediscover.com** and enter this book's unique code.

BOOK CODE

J893462

EYEDISCOVER brings you optic readalongs that support active learning.

Published by AV² by Weigl
350 5th Avenue, 59th Floor New York, NY 10118
Website: www.eyediscover.com

Library of Congress Control Number: 2017930729

ISBN 978-1-4896-5698-8 (hardcover)

Printed in the United States of America
in Brainerd, Minnesota
1 2 3 4 5 6 7 8 9 0 21 20 19 18 17

082017
020317

Editor: Katie Gillespie
Designer: Mandy Christiansen

Weigl acknowledges Getty Images, iStock, Shutterstock, and Dreamstime as the primary image suppliers for this title.

EYEDISCOVER provides enriched content, optimized for tablet use, that supplements and complements this book. EYEDISCOVER books strive to create inspired learning and engage young minds in a total learning experience.

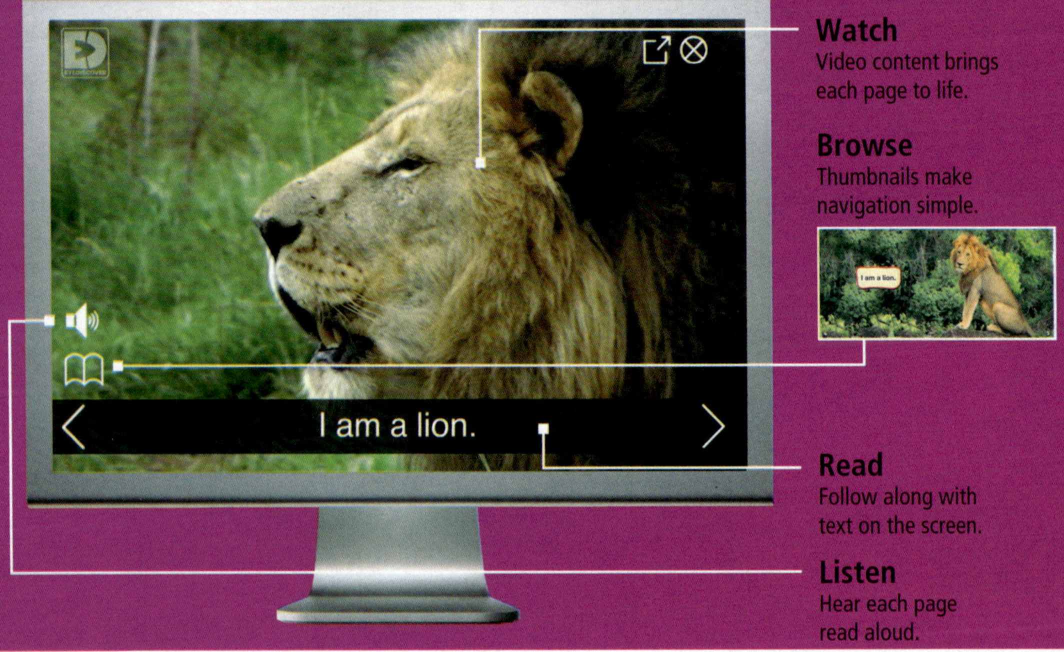

Watch
Video content brings each page to life.

Browse
Thumbnails make navigation simple.

Read
Follow along with text on the screen.

Listen
Hear each page read aloud.

Your EYEDISCOVER Optic Readalongs come alive with...

Audio
Listen to the entire book read aloud.

Video
High resolution videos turn each spread into an optic readalong.

OPTIMIZED FOR

- TABLETS
- WHITEBOARDS
- COMPUTERS
- AND MUCH MORE!

STARS

In this book, you will learn about

- how long stars live
- which star is the brightest
- which star is closest to Earth

and much more!

Earth's home is the Milky Way galaxy. It is made of hundreds of billions of stars.

6

Stars are burning balls of gas that make heat and light. We see starlight in the night sky.

On a clear night, we can see about 2,500 different stars in the sky.

The Sun is our closest star. Without its heat and light, there would be no life on Earth.

Sirius

The brightest star we can see in the sky is Sirius. It is one of the closest stars to Earth.

Stars can live for up to 10 billion years. When some stars die, they make an explosion called a supernova.

Stars can guide people. The North Star is in the same place every night. It shows which way is north.

When you look at the stars, you can sometimes see patterns. We call these patterns constellations.

There are many well-known constellations in the sky. They include Pisces, Taurus, and Orion.

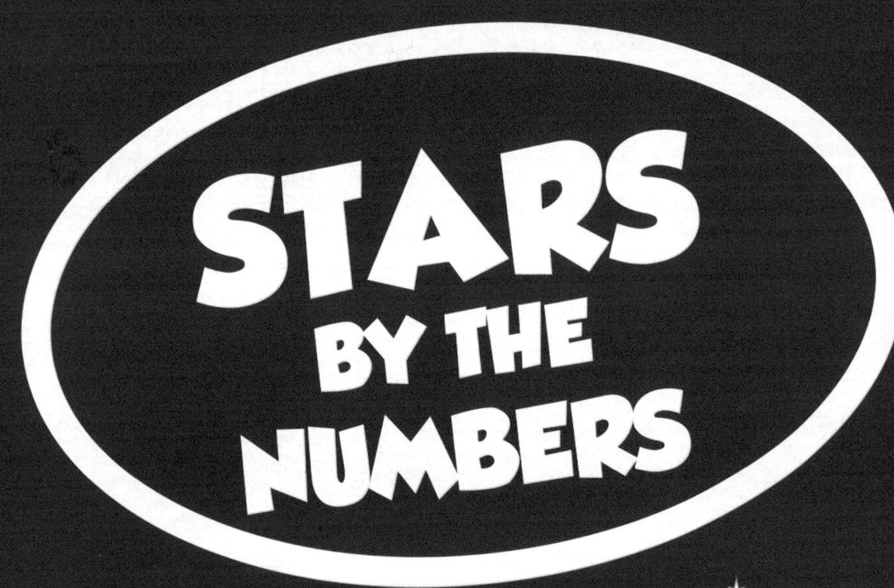

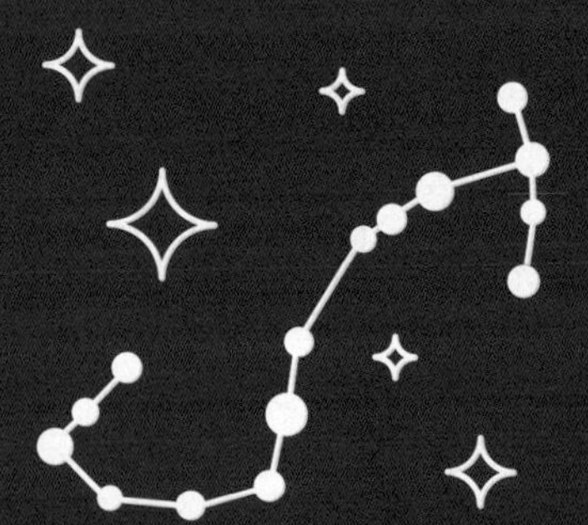

There are **88 official constellations** in the sky.

Deneb

The star **Deneb** can be seen from Earth, even though it is **19 quadrillion miles away**. (30 quadrillion kilometers)

A star's surface can be **more than 90,000° Fahrenheit.** (50,000° Celsius)

Some **stars** could be the **same age** as the universe.

It takes **4.2 years** for **light** from the **second-closest** star to Earth to **reach us**.

Scientists think there might be as many as **300 sextillion stars in the universe**.

KEY WORDS

Research has shown that as much as 65 percent of all written material published in English is made up of 300 words. These 300 words cannot be taught using pictures or learned by sounding them out. They must be recognized by sight. This book contains 55 common sight words to help young readers improve their reading fluency and comprehension. This book also teaches young readers several important content words, such as proper nouns. These words are paired with pictures to aid in learning and improve understanding.

Page	Sight Words First Appearance
4	Earth, home, is, it, made, of, the
7	and, are, in, light, make, night, see, that, we
9	a, about, can, different, on
10	be, its, life, no, our, there, without, would
13	one, to
15	an, for, live, some, they, up, when, years
16	every, people, place, same, shows, way, which
19	at, call, look, sometimes, these, you
21	known, many, well

Page	Content Words First Appearance
4	billions, hundreds, Milky Way galaxy, stars
7	balls, gas, heat, sky, starlight
10	Sun
13	Sirius
15	explosion, supernova
16	north, North Star
19	constellations, patterns
21	Orion, Pisces, Taurus

Watch
Video content brings each page to life.

Browse
Thumbnails make navigation simple.

Read
Follow along with text on the screen.

Listen
Hear each page read aloud.

Go to www.eyediscover.com and enter this book's unique code.

BOOK CODE

J893462